napkin theology

napkin theology

a simple way to share sacred truth

Mike Hilson

wesleyan
publishing
house

Indianapolis, Indiana

Copyright © 2011 by Mike Hilson
Published by Wesleyan Publishing House
Indianapolis, Indiana 46250
Printed in the United States of America
ISBN: 978-0-89827-496-7

Library of Congress Cataloging-in-Publication Data

Hilson, Mike.
    Napkin theology : a simple way to share sacred truth / Mike Hilson.
        p. cm.
    Includes bibliographical references (p.).
    ISBN 978-0-89827-496-7
    1. Discipling (Christianity) 2. Conversation--Religious aspects--Christianity.
    I. Title.
    BV4520.H55 2011
    253.5--dc23
                                    2011022859

Contents

Introduction

Making the Complex Simple

The work of a theologian is to use the full extent of his or her intellect to explain the simple love of God for mankind with whatever degree of complexity is necessary to do the job. The work of a pastor is to explain the complex theologies of God in simple ways. The work of each is important, but the audiences are very different.

The theologian melds his or her study of God into every conceivable philosophical and rational construct so that every question can be dealt with to some predetermined point of satisfaction. In doing so, the theologian speaks to the intellects and elites, gaining entry for the science of knowing God into the academic discussion.

The pastor presents the truth of God's good news to a world in need of a Savior. His or her words are chosen to reach the widest audience possible. While theologically sound, the pastor's communication of the gospel must be easily received, since its purpose is to make the gospel of Christ available to all mankind.

Both tasks are formidable. The pastor still aims to speak the truth in a way that has intellectual integrity. The theologian seeks to speak in a way that can be comprehended by many. In other words, it is the goal of both to speak to the world in understandable and acceptable terms. The purpose of this book is to use simple analogy as an introduction to complex theology. In doing this, we will equip those who disciple others to deal with one of the difficult realities of proclaiming biblical truth today.

During the twenty-plus years that I have been in ministry, one of the questions haunting me, and so many others like me, is how to teach complex theology to people who often will only give you a few minutes of their time. Unfortunately, some have simply given up on teaching theology because they are convinced that people are not interested. That is an incorrect conclusion. Many people have an interest in learning more about the theology of Christ, though they consider themselves too busy to take the time for serious study, and at times are turned off by Christians who don't know or live what they believe. People are *not* interested in wasting time listening to uninformed believers.

This leads to the reality that a Christian will often have little more than a lunch meeting in which to explain his or her belief in God or some other aspect of Christian theology. Often a person will be caught with nothing more than a pen and napkin with which to do the eternal work of the kingdom. So the great question becomes, "How does the person who disciples others teach these deep, meaningful concepts in a way that is both understandable and repeatable?" If theology on a napkin in five minutes or less is what today's culture is demanding, let's consider how we can do that. While it is not going to be a full explanation or a sufficient argument, it will be a starting point, and if that is all we have to work with at the moment, we had better be ready.

Dogma, Doctrine, and Opinion

Christianity has existed for more than two thousand years. Over that time, the thought and belief systems of Christians have become well developed through scholarly conversation and debate. A variety of ideas or theologies have arisen about the proper understanding of God, Jesus, salvation, and Scripture. These ideas or theologies have often been hotly debated, and some are still debated to this day. Some ideas have been rejected as heresy (contrary to proper biblical teaching), and others have been separated into doctrinal categories as debates that cannot be definitively resolved.

However, some ideas have risen above the debate to form the core of Christian faith. These ideas transcend denominational lines and even the deep fissures between Roman Catholic, Eastern Orthodox, and Protestant Christianity. These ideas have become the central theologies of Christianity. They are universally accepted beliefs that define the word *Christian*. To reject these beliefs is to stray from the faith of the Bible. To reject these beliefs is to reject Christianity and the good news of biblical truth.

The best way to describe what we will study is to understand the difference between three terms:

- *Dogma*—Written in Blood: Items of biblical faith that are universally accepted as true and necessary to the faith.
- *Doctrine*—Written in Ink: Items of biblical faith that are honestly contested among well-meaning, biblically centered believers in Jesus Christ.
- *Opinion*—Written in Pencil: Items of biblical faith that are not firmly based in the teaching of Scripture or the tradition of the church.

Understanding the roots of our faith and the reasons why we embrace certain truths strengthens our faith. We gain courage in the knowledge that ours is a historic faith and that our understanding of God is part of a pattern of thought that has been tested and tried for nearly twenty-one centuries. We learn of a God who is loving and capable, holy and forgiving, demanding and empowering, one and three. We learn of a forgiveness that is neither deserved nor earned, but rather is freely given by the loving God of heaven. We learn of a word of truth given to us through the Holy Scripture that is able to encourage, teach, comfort, and sustain us in our life journey. We learn of a body of believers known as the church that is God's instrument for reaching a world in need of his love, power, forgiveness, and truth.

Using This Book

Using this book is simple. Each chapter addresses a single point of theology and approaches it from a variety of perspectives.

The Conversation

Each chapter begins with a sample conversation that illustrates a teachable moment, a situation in which the truths explored in the chapter are particularly relevant.

Usually, these are based on actual conversations I've had with people learning about the Christian faith.

Teachable Questions

Each sample conversation is followed by a set of teachable questions. These are questions that indicate an open door to teachable moments on the point of theology to be covered in the chapter.

Please be aware that many Christians over the years have been content to offer prepackaged slogans in response to people's genuine questions about the faith; much damage to people's faith has resulted from Christians who memorize and recite such slogans. That is not the purpose of suggesting teachable questions. Instead, they are examples of the kinds of questions people ask that might be an invitation into an honest conversation. The goal is to get you thinking about situations in which you might share the information that is presented and specific ways you might introduce the topic and have a real conversation with a friend.

The Napkin

After the sample conversation and questions, you will find a simple image that can easily be reproduced with a pen or pencil on a napkin (or whatever is handy). Each image is accompanied by a short explanation of the theological principle that it portrays.

The Truth

These images are then followed by a deeper, more detailed explanation of the principle, one that is easy to understand and communicate. This explanation offers a scriptural, historical, and theological basis for the theological truth illustrated by the image. It provides further background information that might be useful for your conversations. This section is written with the person being discipled in mind.

The Exercise

Each chapter concludes with a brief exercise to help you practice or further search out the truth represented by the image.

To communicate our theology well, we need to have a thorough understanding of the doctrine and its intellectual basis. For this reason, each chapter includes more information than could probably be shared in a five-minute discussion over lunch with a pen and napkin. The study in each chapter is not a script to be used verbatim, but a resource for understanding and communicating the truth. The better you come to understanding each principle, the more effectively you will be able to explain them in a short time frame.

Also, keep in mind that this book is not designed to provide new ammunition for your next "battle" with unbelieving friends. These are truths for believers to understand and internalize. As we embrace the truth, it changes our life. And that life change can open the door for discussions with others about the God we serve. We don't argue our way to the salvation of others; we win the right to speak by being what our theology says we are.

One last note: Please remember that these quick, easy images are not meant to be complete or perfect in their ability to explain these vast ideas about God and our relationship with him. Hopefully, they will provide good starting points. And with the help of the Holy Spirit, they will form the basis for many open, honest conversations with others about the truth of the good news of the Bible.

For since the creation of the world God's invisible qualities—
his eternal power and divine nature—have been clearly seen, being
understood from what has been made, so that men are without excuse.

—Romans 1:20

1 The God of the Bible

The God of the Bible
is indescribably
great. He has
chosen to reveal
his person and
greatness to us.

The Conversation

"So, don't all religions serve the same God? And
wouldn't that mean that all paths lead to heaven?"

The question came at me out of the blue. I was in
college at the time and had not encountered many people
who didn't already believe in God. In fact, being raised
in a strong Christian family and community, most people
I knew believed in the Christian God of the Bible. I was

taken aback by the question, and simply answered, "Well, no. Of course not."

That was the extent of it. Instead of being able to defend my sincerely held conviction, I could only react defensively. Although I knew that the God of the Bible was different from all those other gods, I wasn't certain how he was different, or how I knew that he was different.

Today, I would answer that question differently. I would not become defensive, because I have learned that God does not need me to defend him. Instead, I understand my role to be introducing the people around me to him.

What other god is known to have personally arrived on the planet to live with and die for his creation? What other god is known to act and react out of a deep love for his creation? What other god is known to be intricately and personally interested and involved in the lives of human beings all around the planet? The God of the Bible is so great and absolutely unique that a simple introduction to him and explanation of why he is different will suffice.

Teachable Questions

Isn't the God of the Bible the same as the god of the Koran?

How is your God different from any other god?

Don't all roads lead to the same God?

Don't all religions teach the same things about God?

Why should I choose the God of the Bible over any of the other gods?

The Napkin

The napkin is empty.

The reason for this is simple. No images of God are sufficient and therefore none should be attempted. To attempt to draw an image representing God would limit our understanding of the nature and power of an indescribably powerful and great God. There are no lines big enough, no colors shocking enough, no images impressive enough, and no thoughts vast enough to depict God.

This does not mean that paintings, for example, that attempt to depict the actions of God are somehow sinful. Our empty napkin is simply a way to illustrate the unexplainable-ness of the God we serve. Nothing describes the indescribable. So nothing may explain it best.

The Truth

Sing to the LORD a new song; sing to the LORD, all the earth. Sing to the LORD, praise his name; proclaim his salvation day after day. Declare his glory among the nations, his marvelous deeds among all peoples. For great is the LORD and most worthy of praise; he is to be feared above all gods. For all the gods of the nations are idols, but the LORD made the heavens. Splendor and majesty are before him; strength and glory are in his sanctuary. Ascribe to the LORD, O families of nations, ascribe to the LORD glory and strength. Ascribe to the LORD the glory due his name; bring an offering and come into his courts. Worship the LORD in the splendor of his holiness; tremble before him, all the earth. Say among the nations, "The LORD reigns." The world is firmly established, it cannot be moved; he will judge the peoples with equity. Let the heavens rejoice, let the earth be glad; let the sea resound, and all that is in it; let the fields be jubilant, and everything in them. Then all the trees of the forest will sing for joy; they will sing before the LORD, for he comes, he comes to judge the earth. He will judge the world in righteousness and the peoples in his truth.

—Psalm 96

While every religious system believes in some kind of god and has its own understanding of that god's nature and identity, these gods are not the same as the God of the Bible.

Contrary to popular thought, all gods are not equal.

While the gods of other religions are often seen as powerful, and in some cases as all-powerful, they are often understood to be self-serving, unapproachable, or inconceivable. The God of the Bible, however, is not self-serving. He is approachable and has made himself known to us by becoming one of us. The God of the Bible is unique in his desire for a relationship with his creation. God reveals himself to us in two ways. Theologians call the two ways general and special revelation.

General Revelation

God revealed himself to us through the creation in which he placed us. The apostle Paul asserted this in the first chapter of his letter to the Romans; Paul emphasized that no one has any excuse for failing to recognize God through his creation (Rom. 1:18–20). We can see God in the incredible balance and intricate complexities of nature. Although many have argued that nature came to us through a chaotic series of random events, the Bible has the story right: "In the beginning God . . ." (Gen. 1:1). The very complexity of nature itself demands the existence of a Grand Designer.

That Designer is God.

General revelation also includes what we can know from human nature. As C. S. Lewis argued in *Mere Christianity*, the fact that virtually all of humanity recognizes a consistent, personal moral code speaks to the existence of an overarching moral presence.[1] That presence is God. The complexity of nature and the uniformity of human moral expectations argue clearly for the existence of God, "so that men are without excuse" (Rom. 1:20).

Special Revelation

Special revelation is when God uses means other than nature to reveal himself to his creation. God is described for us in the Bible. His character and nature are revealed to us. We find numerous pictures of who God is and what he does in Scripture. One of Scripture's primary goals is to provide a clear understanding of the God we serve.

In addition to the Bible, God's special revelation is also seen in the person of Jesus Christ. Jesus is God incarnate, God in the flesh. He is the image of God among us. In giving us Jesus to be our Savior, God also gave us Jesus to be the special image of himself.

Another place we see God's special revelation is in the narrative of human history. God has intervened in history in ways that are not otherwise explainable. His miraculous intervention, both personally and globally, is a special revelation of himself to us.

While most people may be content to speak of some distant, indescribable, unapproachable, inconceivable god, as Christians, we have more. Our view of God grows as we read through the pages of the Bible. We find a God who is so much more than we could have ever hoped for or expected. We find the eternal God, Creator, Redeemer, Provider, and Ruler. He is not only a god who was or will be, but a God who is, now and forever.

The Exercise

List some examples of what you would describe as God's general and special revelation.

General Revelation:

Special Revelation:

Then Jesus came to them and said, "All authority in heaven and on earth has been given to me. Therefore go and make disciples of all nations, baptizing them in the name of the Father and of the Son and of the Holy Spirit, and teaching them to obey everything I have commanded you. And surely I am with you always, to the very end of the age."
—Matthew 28:18–20

2
The Trinity

The God of the Bible is described as one God in three persons. From the beginning, the church has understood God as being in full community within himself.

The Conversation

"OK, I understand God, and I think I understand that Jesus is God's Son, and then the Holy Spirit is like the presence of God on earth, but what is this about a Trinity? Aren't these three different people? And if so, how can they be one?"

That question has come up many times over the years. Generally, it comes from one of two types of people. First are the people who are genuinely curious. They have come to faith in Christ and are trying to understand that faith, but they find the doctrine of the Trinity to be difficult to understand. With this type of person, the discussion can be real, and there is a hopeful path to understanding. While the Trinity is by far the most difficult of all Christian doctrines, it is still a sensible one, if we are willing to accept God as "entirely other" than us. So for this person, the conversation would be very worthwhile. A simple affirmation of the person's desire to wrestle with the issue followed by a discussion of the napkin graphic can help bring understanding and peace.

Then there are people who ask this question to play a game of "gotcha." They are familiar with the teachings of the Christian faith, but they resist accepting the Bible and Christianity. Such people are often trying to assert an intellectual dominance; they believe they can trap you in this discussion. Once you recognize that you are dealing with someone who is playing games, you can kindly and with justification remove yourself from the conversation with a response like: "You know, to have faith sometimes does just require faith." There is no need to argue and certainly no need to become angry. Remember, even Jesus encountered people who listened only for the purpose of picking a fight. Simply move on and pray for the Holy Spirit to move in the person's heart at sometime in the future.

Teachable Questions

If Jesus is God's Son, when was he created?

If the Holy Spirit is a way of talking about the presence of God, why do you call him a person?

Does the Bible ever talk about the Trinity?

Did Jesus really claim to be God?

Does the Bible ever really call the Holy Spirit God?

The Napkin

"God the Father, God the Son, and God the Holy Spirit" is a common phrase that you have probably heard in church or at least at weddings and funerals.

Some may see it as nothing more than a formal way of addressing God at formal occasions. But in reality, it is a key part of understanding who God is and how he works within and among us.

The doctrine of the Trinity is central to our ability to rightly read the Bible and what it says about God.

As we consider this image, remember that the concept of the Trinity is one that is not easily understood. When we talk about the Trinity, we are talking about the mystery of God. He is entirely other than we are. He is different in the most powerful and fundamental ways. Even while we are made in his image, he is so much more. So, for him to be indescribable, or beyond our ability to understand, is simply him being God.

The Truth

In the Great Commission (Matt. 28:18–20), Jesus gave the church its marching orders: "All authority in heaven and on earth has been given to me. Therefore go and make disciples of all nations." But then, in his instruction to baptize these new disciples, he hinted at a mystery that has defined the Christian church understanding of God ever since: "baptizing them in the name of the Father and of the Son and of the Holy Spirit."

At first glance, one might wonder what the big deal is. To those who have been exposed to the Bible and the traditions of the church, the phrase seems perfectly normal. Yet to those original disciples who heard it for the first time on that day, it must have seemed earth shattering. It would be blasphemy (an offense to God) to baptize in any name other than God's. So what was Jesus asking his disciples to do? Why would he instruct them to baptize in a name other than that of Almighty God? The answer is that he would not. With this command, Jesus was revealing the existence of a reality that the church now calls the Trinity: God in three persons.

To better understand the nature of this revelation, consider this foundational verse, which was one of the most frequently recited verses in the disciples' culture: "Hear, O Israel: The LORD our God, the LORD is one" (Deut. 6:4). From the very beginning, the God of Israel was defined by his oneness. There were not many gods: there was only one. But Jesus revolutionized the way his disciples, and later the church, saw God. In the gospel of John, Jesus began to lay the groundwork for this deeper understanding of who God is. "Jesus answered, 'I am the way and the truth and the life. No one comes to the Father except through me. If you really knew me, you would know my Father as well. From now on, you do know him and have seen him'" (John 14:6–7). Here, and at other points in Scripture, Jesus claimed the title and position of God.

Jesus then complicated matters further when he said, "All this I have spoken while still with you. But the Counselor, the Holy Spirit, whom the Father will send in my name, will teach you all things and will remind you of everything I have said to you" (John 14:25–26).

Jesus explained that God would send this Counselor to stand in his place and lead the disciples and ultimately the church in Jesus' absence. The importance of this third person, known as the Holy Spirit, is further explained by Jesus in the gospel of Matthew, where he declared, "Anyone who speaks a word against the Son of Man will be forgiven, but anyone who speaks against the Holy Spirit will not be forgiven, either in this age or in the age to come" (Matt. 12:32). Jesus firmly established the truth that the Holy Spirit is truly God.

How do we reconcile these seemingly incompatible teachings of Scripture that God is one and that Jesus and the Holy Spirit are also God? The church, while immediately accepting these teachings at face value, took many years to formally explain in writing how they are to be reconciled. The church included teaching the Trinity in the Apostles' Creed, which dates to the second century, and formalized the theology at the Council of Constantinople, which took place in A.D. 381. The image at the beginning of this section is an adaptation of one created by the Cappadocian Fathers (Basil the Great, Gregory of Nyssa, and Gregory of Nazianzus; three bishops from what is known today as Turkey) who were influential at the Council of Constantinople. The image helps clarify many important points about the Trinitarian nature of God.

You can see the texts from two of the earliest attempts of the church to define this challenging teaching: the Apostles' Creed and the Nicene Creed.

The Apostles' Creed

I believe in God the Father almighty,
maker of heaven and earth:

And in Jesus Christ his only Son our Lord,
who was conceived by the Holy Ghost,
born of the Virgin Mary,
suffered under Pontius Pilate,
was crucified, dead and buried.
He descended into hell;
the third day he rose again from the dead;
he ascended into heaven,
and sitteth on the right hand of God the
Father almighty;
from thence he shall come to judge the quick
and the dead.

I believe in the Holy Ghost;
the holy catholic Church;
the communion of saints;
the forgiveness of sins;
the resurrection of the body,
and the life everlasting.
Amen.[1]

The Nicene Creed (A.D. 381)

We believe in one God,
the Father, the Almighty,
maker of heaven and earth,
of all that is,
seen and unseen.

We believe in one Lord, Jesus Christ,
the only Son of God,
eternally begotten of the Father,
God from God, Light from Light,
true God from true God,
begotten, not made,
of one Being with the Father;
through him all things were made.
For us and for our salvation he came
down from heaven,
was incarnate from the Holy Spirit and
the Virgin Mary
and was made man.
For our sake he was crucified under Pontius Pilate;
he suffered death and was buried.
On the third day he rose again
in accordance with the Scriptures;
he ascended into heaven
and is seated at the right hand of the Father.
He will come again in glory to judge the living
and the dead,
and his kingdom will have no end.

We believe in the Holy Spirit,
the Lord, the giver of life,
who proceeds from the Father and the Son,
who with the Father and the Son is
worshipped and glorified.
who has spoken through the prophets.
We believe in one holy catholic and
apostolic Church.
We acknowledge one baptism for the
forgiveness of sins.
We look for the resurrection of the dead,
and the life of the world to come.
Amen.[2]

From these two statements of faith, we can already begin to see a balance emerging in the church's understanding of the Trinity. There are four major points to remember:

1. There is only one God.
2. The Father, Son, and Spirit are all individual persons.
3. The unity of the three in one is a divine mystery.
4. The doctrine of the Trinity is a theological necessity.

The Exercise

In light of all that we have seen, and considering our graphic, fill in the following blanks:

The Father is _____.

The Father is not _____ or _____.

The Son is _____.

The Son is not _____ or _____.

The Spirit is _____.

The Spirit is not _____ or _____.

Twelve key passages on the Trinity are:

1. Jesus' Baptism—Matthew 3:16
2. The Baptismal Formula—Matthew 28:19
3. The Prologue of John—John 1:1–4
4. Jesus' Farewell Discourse—John 14:26; 15:26

5. The Varieties of Gifts—1 Corinthians 12:4–6

6. Paul's Apostolic Benediction—2 Corinthians 13:14

7. The Ephesian Formula—Ephesians 2:18

8. Paul's Description of a Servant—Philippians 2:5–11

9. Introduction of Colossians—Colossians 1:3–8, 12–19

10. Summary of Salvation History—Hebrews 1:1–5

11. Johannine Letters—1 John 3:23—4:3

12. The Apocalypse Salutation—Revelation 1:4–6

3

God the Father

We were created

by God who is

above us and

great beyond our

comprehension.

The Conversation

"So, what is God like?"

This can be a frightening question to answer when you are not prepared for it. When we are called on to describe the God of the universe, we are given a great responsibility. People want to know the truth. They want to know if God can be trusted, admired, reached, and understood. They want to know God.

Since my college days, I have been attached to a phrase: God is entirely other. Any conversation about who God is must start there. All too often we try to explain God in human terms, which is understandable. After all, being human is the only reference point we have. But any conversation about who God is must start with a realization that he is entirely other than we are. So, I suggest beginning conversations about the nature of God by pointing out how great and awesome the God of the Bible really is. Start with a picture of God that is awesome and out there, and then zoom in on that image to help the person see a God that is reachable, loving, and concerned for us, his creation.

Teachable Questions

What is God like?

Can I trust God to hear my prayers?

Is God kind and forgiving?

Did God make everything?

Will God take care of me?

What does the Bible really say about God?

The Father above me, Jesus beside me, the Spirit inside me.

The Napkin

The drawing for this chapter also forms the basis for the next two chapters. It shows the work of each member of the Trinity in the life of an individual, beginning with God the Father.

God the Father is over me.

He is Creator. He is Ruler. He is King. He is Lord.

He is more. He is stronger. He is everywhere.

God the Father is over me.

We have a Father God who is more powerful than we can imagine. He is always able to take care of us and our needs. Since the One who rules our world loves us, we can live in peace and security by placing our faith and trust in him.

God the Father is over us.

The Truth

The Bible not only explains what God does, but also who he is. The terms used to describe God can be divided into two categories. *Economic language* is used to describe what God does, and *immanent language* is used to describe who God is. This is a small but important distinction, because no one act of God can completely describe what he does. Likewise, no one characteristic of God can completely describe who he is. So it is important to remember the distinction between who God is and what he does.

While there is evidence in the Old Testament of God the Son (Jesus) and God the Holy Spirit, the majority of the Old Testament describes God the Father. The Old Testament does us a great service by using different names for God to describe his attributes. These names give us our first understanding of the nature and character of God.

The various names that describe God in the Old Testament are built around three basic names for God:

- Elohim—God the strong creator
- Jehovah—the Lord or self-existent one who reveals himself to us
- Adonai—Lord or master

From these three basic concepts come the various other names that reveal God's character. These three basic names speak solely to the power and otherness of God. If we knew God only in these three names, we might find him to be frightening and threatening. A God who is known simply as all-powerful (Elohim), self-existent (Jehovah), and master of everything (Adonai) would probably strike fear into the human heart and leave us helpless and hopeless in his presence. But what if we knew more of him? What if, in finding out more about this God who is entirely other, we find that he is also kind, understanding, loving, and forgiving? That is precisely what the people of the Old Testament learned from the names by which God revealed himself.

The Exercise

Consider what we learn from these names of God:

- Jehovah *Roi*—The Lord our shepherd (Ps. 23:1)
- Jehovah *Jireh*—The Lord our provider (Gen. 22:14)
- Jehovah *Shammah*—The Lord is there (Ezek. 48:35)

- Jehovah *Rophe*—The Lord our healer (Ex. 15:26)
- Jehovah *Tsidkenu*—The Lord our righteousness (Jer. 23:6)
- Jehovah *Mekaddishkhem*—The Lord our sanctifier (Ex. 31:13)
- Jehovah *Shalom*—The Lord our peace (Judg. 6:24)

In these names, we begin to gain an understanding of the character of our wonderful God, who can be entirely other while simultaneously being entirely compassionate. God is all powerful; therefore, he is able. God is all loving; therefore, he is good.

Draw a line to match the name to the corresponding Scripture:

Immanent Terms for God the Father (Who God Is)	Scripture
The All-Powerful God	Job 38:1–7
The All-Present God	Romans 11:33–36
The All-Knowing God	Psalm 139:7–12
The Uncreated God	Jeremiah 32:17
The Unequaled God	1 John 3:19–20

Economic Terms for God the Father (What God Does)	Scripture
God the Judge	Exodus 20:1—21:1
God the Creator	2 Samuel 7:22
God the Ruler	Genesis 22:1–14
God the Law Giver	Ezekiel 18:30–32
God the Provider	Genesis 1

"The virgin will be with child and will give
birth to a son, and they will call him Immanuel"—
which means "God with us."
—Matthew 1:23

4
Jesus the Son

Jesus is

God with us.

The Conversation

"Sure, Jesus was a great teacher, but was he really God?"
Most people have heard of the Christmas story and
Jesus' birth. Most have heard of the Easter story and
Jesus' death and resurrection. But many have simply
taken these in the same light as stories about other
great humans who lived and died over the centuries.
They miss or ignore the idea that this man was also God.
And then when confronted with that reality, they hesitate.

If Jesus is human, how can he be God too? Again, the question continues. As in the first discussions in this book, we must begin with the realization that since Jesus is God, he is almost entirely other. But with Jesus, it is different. He is both entirely other and entirely like us. And here is where our conversation gets tough again. I often will share the following statement: Jesus is 100 percent human and 100 percent God; he is the only 200 percent person ever to exist! That statement usually relaxes the tension and allows me to move forward with some of the truth that is found in the remainder of this chapter. Remember, faith sometimes requires faith. And though the Bible gives us ample evidence for everything that the church teaches about Jesus, there is still the issue of faith.

Teachable Questions

Is Jesus God?

If Jesus was born and died, how can he be God?

Why does it matter if we see Jesus as human?

Why does it matter if we see Jesus as God?

What good does a 200 percent person do us?

Does the Bible really say Jesus is God?

Does Jesus really claim to be God?

The Father above me, Jesus beside me, the Spirit inside me.

The Napkin

The drawing for this chapter, which we have already seen in the previous chapter, shows the work of each person of the Trinity in the life of an individual. Here we focus on Jesus, God's Son.

Jesus the Son is beside me.

While, God the Father is entirely other, Jesus is God incarnate. This simply means God in the flesh. Jesus is God with skin.

This truth reminds us that our God understands what we are going through. This truth shows just how much

God loves us—so much that he, Jesus the Son, would come personally to teach us and die for us. And this truth assures us that God paid the price for our sin by becoming one of us.

Jesus the Son came and lived, ate, talked, walked, and died with us.

No other god does that. Jesus is beside us.

The Creed of Nicaea (A.D. 352)

We believe . . . in one Lord Jesus Christ, the Son of God, begotten of the Father . . . of the essence of the Father, God of God, and Light of Light, very God of very God, begotten, not made, being of one substance with the Father; by whom all things were made [in heaven and on earth]; who for us men, and for our salvation, came down and was incarnate and was made man; he suffered, and the third day he rose again, ascended into heaven; from thence he cometh to judge the quick and the dead.[1]

Jesus is human. He was born of a human woman. He ate, slept, cried, tired, bled, and died.

Jesus is God. His birth was announced by angels. He healed the sick, walked on water, fed multitudes with one boy's lunch, brought the dead back to life, and was resurrected from the dead.

Here lies the greatest story of all time. While the two statements—Jesus is human, and Jesus is God—seem contradictory, they are not. Jesus is 100 percent God, and he is 100 percent human. Jesus is God incarnate (God in the flesh). He is, "'Immanuel'—which means 'God with us'" (Matt. 1:23). God's greatest revelation of himself to us is in the person of Jesus, God's Son, the Christ.

Over the centuries, some have argued that Jesus is not fully God and fully man. In fact, the Creed of Nicaea was written at the conclusion of the first Council of Nicaea, which was called to straighten out some false teaching on the person of Jesus. A group led by a man named Arius had decided that Jesus was not fully God. The early church theologians, most notably Athanasius, successfully maintained the historical teaching of the church that Jesus was fully God. Make no mistake, Arius' teaching was not the normal thought of the day. It is clear from Scripture and from the earliest teachings of the church that Jesus was seen as both fully human and fully God. In fact, Jesus himself claimed to be the very image of God among us. Jesus asked, "Don't you know me, Philip, even after I have been among you such a long time? Anyone who has seen me has seen the Father. How can you say, 'Show us the Father'?" (John 14:9).

Furthermore, Jesus laid direct claim to being the Son of God: "They all asked, 'Are you then the Son of God?' He replied, 'You are right in saying I am'" (Luke 22:70).

The Bible is very clear on the divinity and humanity of Jesus the Christ. While some would argue with one side or the other of this issue, the historical tradition of the church has remained firm: Jesus is God. Jesus is human.

Jesus Solves Our Human Problem

Because Jesus was fully human, he could correct the problem that had plagued humanity from the beginning of time: the sin of Adam. The apostle Paul made this clear in his writing to the church at Rome: "Consequently, just as the result of one trespass was condemnation for all men, so also the result of one act of righteousness was justification that brings life for all men. For just as through the disobedience of the one man [Adam] the many were made sinners, so also through the obedience of the one man [Jesus] the many will be made righteous" (Rom. 5:18–19).

Jesus Provides a Human Example

By being perfectly obedient to the law of the Father, Jesus set an example for us for how to live in this world. The apostle Peter said, "To this you were called, because Christ suffered for you, leaving you an example, that you should follow in his steps" (1 Pet. 2:21). The apostle John said, "Whoever claims to live in him must walk as Jesus did" (1 John 2:6).

Jesus Paid the Ultimate Human Price

By living a perfect life, Jesus also set the stage for the ultimate sacrifice for sins. He paid the price for our sinfulness: "Since the children have flesh and blood, [Jesus] too shared in their humanity so that by his death he might destroy him who holds the power of death—that is, the devil—and free those who all their lives were held in slavery by their fear of death" (Heb. 2:14–15).

Jesus the Divine Creator

Because Jesus was fully God, he held the authority to change our situation. The apostle John was so committed to establishing the life-changing truth of a Savior who was truly God that he began his gospel with these words: "In the beginning was the Word [Jesus], and the Word was with God, and the Word was God. He was with God in the beginning. Through him all things were made; without him nothing was made that has been made. In him was life, and that life was the light of men. The light shines in the darkness, but the darkness has not understood it" (John 1:1–5).

Jesus the Divine Healer

Because Jesus was fully God, he had authority over sickness and demon possession. "Jesus went throughout Galilee, teaching in their synagogues, preaching the good news of the kingdom, and healing every disease and sickness among the people. News about him spread all over Syria, and people brought to him all who were ill with various diseases, those suffering severe pain, the demon-possessed, those having seizures, and the paralyzed, and he healed them" (Matt. 4:23–24).

Jesus the Divine Master of Nature

Because Jesus was fully God, he also exercised power over the forces of nature. "Without warning, a furious storm came up on the lake, so that the waves swept over the boat. But Jesus was sleeping. The disciples went and woke him, saying, 'Lord, save us! We're going to drown!' He replied, 'You of little faith, why are you so afraid?' Then he got up and rebuked the winds and the waves, and it was completely calm. The men were amazed and asked, 'What kind of man is this? Even the winds and the waves obey him!'" (Matt. 8:24–27).

Jesus the Divine Master of Life

Because Jesus was fully God, he exercised authority even over death and the grave. "Soon afterward, Jesus went to a town called Nain, and his disciples and a large crowd went along with him. As he approached the town gate, a dead person was being carried out—the only son of his mother, and she was a widow. And a large crowd from the town was with her. When the Lord saw her, his heart went out to her and he said, 'Don't cry.' Then he went up and touched the coffin, and those carrying it stood still. He said, 'Young man, I say to you, get up!' The dead man sat up and began to talk, and Jesus gave him back to his mother" (Luke 7:11–15).

Jesus the Divine Intercessor

Now, since the example has been set and the price has been paid, Jesus speaks for us to God the Father and is our advocate in heaven. "For there is one God and one mediator between God and men, the man Christ Jesus, who gave himself as a ransom for all men—the testimony given in its proper time" (1 Tim. 2:5–6).

The Exercise

Consider the following verses, and indicate whether they speak to the humanity or divinity of Jesus the Christ:

- Hebrews 1:1–3   Humanity   Divinity
- Matthew 4:1–2   Humanity   Divinity
- John 8:58   Humanity   Divinity
- Mark 13:32   Humanity   Divinity
- Hebrews 13:8   Humanity   Divinity
- Mark 14:60–62   Humanity   Divinity
- Luke 22:39–44   Humanity   Divinity
- Mark 8:27–30   Humanity   Divinity
- 1 John 1:1   Humanity   Divinity
- Acts 7:54–60   Humanity   Divinity

> But the Counselor, the Holy Spirit, whom the
> Father will send in my name, will teach you all things and
> will remind you of everything I have said to you.
> —John 14:26

5
God the Holy Spirit

God created us.

God saved us.

God lives

within us!

The Conversation

"Isn't the Holy Spirit, or the Spirit of God, like the spirit of Christmas? Or like the force in *Star Wars*?"

Wow, I don't like that comparison. But it does come up. People often mistake the Holy Spirit as some impersonal force, so they naturally think of the spirit of Christmas that is often symbolized by Santa Claus or the force found by Luke Skywalker in *Star Wars*. Most of the time people don't mean this to be offensive; it is just the way they view the Holy Spirit.

The Holy Spirit is not at all like the spirit of Christmas or the force in *Star Wars*. The spirit of Christmas is a phrase that simply describes a mood that people are supposed to get into around December each year. The Holy Spirit is a person, not a mood. The force in *Star Wars* is some flighty, impersonal strength that just shows up in certain people who are somehow special. The Holy Spirit is a person, and his role is to touch, lead, and assist everyone, not just a special, chosen few.

The Holy Spirit is more than some vague sense of the presence of God, as if God were a ghost that made us feel his presence in the dark shadows of a nighttime hallway. The Holy Spirit is the third person of the Trinity and has some special work to do. His work is especially significant because it directly touches our everyday lives.

Teachable Questions

Isn't the Holy Spirit just kind of a sense of God's presence around us?

Is the Holy Spirit really different from God?

If we have God the Father and Jesus the Son, why would we need the Holy Spirit?

Does the Bible really talk about the Holy Spirit?

Does the Bible really call the Holy Spirit God?

Is the Holy Spirit just a New Testament thing?
What does the Holy Spirit do?

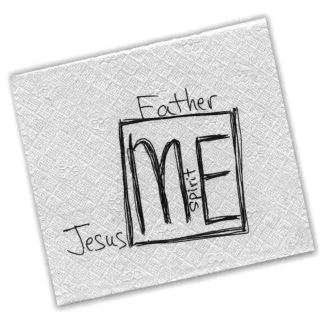

The Father above me, Jesus beside me, the Spirit inside me.

The Napkin

The drawing for this chapter, which we have already seen in two previous chapters, shows the work of each person of the Trinity in the life of an individual. Here we focus on the Holy Spirit.

God the Father is over me. Jesus the Son is beside me. The Holy Spirit is in me.

If we only had the Father above us, then God might seem unreachable and terrifying.

If we only had the Father and Jesus, they might still seem distant, since Jesus returned to heaven.

But with the Holy Spirit, God is with us always!

God is not only with us, he is in us.

He is comforting, leading, teaching, and speaking to us.

The Spirit is in us.

The Truth

The least studied and most misunderstood person of the Trinity is the Holy Spirit. While the role of God the Father and God the Son are easier to understand, it is often difficult for us to understand the role of the Holy Spirit. One way to make sense of it is to understand the main responsibilities of each person of the Trinity, as the church has traditionally defined them.

- God the Father—Creator
- God the Son (Jesus)—Redeemer
- God the Holy Spirit—Sustainer

While God the Father created us and God the Son redeemed us, it is the role of the Holy Spirit to sustain our lives here on earth. The very existence of the earth is sustained by the person of the Holy Spirit.

> By his breath the skies became fair; his hand
> pierced the gliding serpent. And these are but
> the outer fringe of his works; how faint the
> whisper we hear of him! Who then
> can understand the thunder of his power?
> —Job 26:13–14

While the Holy Spirit has been at work in our world since the beginning of time, our perception of him has changed as our understanding of God has changed. Therefore we will take a look at the work of the Holy Spirit in three phases: in the Old Testament, during the life of Christ, and in the New Testament.

The Work of the Holy Spirit in the Old Testament

Creation. From the beginning, the Holy Spirit has been part of God's work. In Genesis 1:2, the presence of the Holy Spirit is noted: "Now the earth was formless and empty, darkness was over the surface of the deep, and the Spirit of God was hovering over the waters." Job saw the Holy Spirit as his Creator: "The Spirit of God has made me; the breath of the Almighty gives me life" (Job 33:4). The work of the Holy Spirit in creation is also suggested in Psalm 104:30: "When you send your Spirit, they are created, and you renew the face of the earth."

Inspiration. God the Holy Spirit has given humanity understanding of himself and the world around him from the beginning of time. Through the Holy Spirit, we gain understanding: "But it is the spirit in a man, the breath of the Almighty, that gives him understanding" (Job 32:8). The inspiration of the Holy Spirit is an absolute necessity for godly and visionary leadership even today. The Holy Spirit also inspired great tasks. One such example is: "Samson went down to Timnah together with his father and mother. As they approached the vineyards of Timnah, suddenly a young lion came roaring toward him. The Spirit of the LORD came upon him in power so that he tore the lion apart with his bare hands as he might have torn a young goat" (Judg. 14:5–6).

Prophecy. The prophetic word of the Holy Spirit has always been one of the most prominent of his roles in human history. This pattern begins as a way for God to lead and speak to the nation of Israel. "For many years you were patient with them. By your Spirit you admonished them through your prophets. Yet they paid no attention, so you handed them over to the neighboring peoples" (Neh. 9:30). It continued with God revealing how the nation of Israel would be destroyed (Hos. 1:1–9) and ultimately how the Messiah would come to earth (Isa. 7:14).

The Work of the Holy Spirit in the life of Christ

Conception. The virgin birth of Jesus Christ was enabled by the power and presence of the Holy Spirit. The angel Gabriel told Mary what was about to happen to her: "The Holy Spirit will come upon you, and the power of the

Most High will overshadow you. So the holy one to be born will be called the Son of God" (Luke 1:35).

Testing. After the birth and later the baptism of Jesus, the Bible records that, "Jesus was led by the Spirit into the desert to be tempted by the devil" (Matt. 4:1). While the devil was the source of the temptation, it was the Spirit who put him to the test.

Ministry. The ministry of Jesus was prophesied and empowered by the Holy Spirit. He attested to that fact by quoting from the prophet Isaiah: "The Spirit of the Lord is on me, because he has anointed me to preach good news to the poor. He has sent me to proclaim freedom for the prisoners and recovery of sight for the blind, to release the oppressed, to proclaim the year of the Lord's favor. . . . Today this scripture is fulfilled in your hearing" (Luke 4:18–19, 21).

Resurrection. The Holy Spirit also played a role in the resurrection of Jesus, as the apostle Paul pointed out: "And if the Spirit of him who raised Jesus from the dead is living in you, he who raised Christ from the dead will also give life to your mortal bodies through his Spirit, who lives in you" (Rom. 8:11).

The Work of the Holy Spirit in the New Testament

Scripture. "All Scripture is God-breathed and is useful for teaching, rebuking, correcting and training in righteousness, so that the man of God may be thoroughly equipped for every good work" (2 Tim. 3:16–17). In this statement, the apostle Paul defined the importance of Scripture, but he did more by describing Scripture as "God-breathed." He referred to work of the Holy Spirit who inspired and maintains the accuracy of Scripture.

The Church. The presence of the Holy Spirit marked the creation of the church and empowers the mission of the church. Acts describes the birth of the church on the day of Pentecost: "When the day of Pentecost came, they were all together in one place. Suddenly a sound like the blowing of a violent wind came from heaven and filled the whole house where they were sitting. They saw what seemed to be tongues of fire that separated and came to rest on each of them. All of them were filled with the Holy Spirit and began to speak in other tongues as the Spirit enabled them" (Acts 2:1–4).

As the church has developed, the Holy Spirit has enabled its members to accomplish the will of God the Father through the use of spiritual gifts that are freely given by the Holy Spirit:

Now to each one the manifestation of the Spirit is given for the common good. To one there is given through the Spirit the message of wisdom, to another the message of knowledge by means of the same Spirit, to another faith by the same Spirit, to another gifts of healing by that one Spirit, to another miraculous powers, to another prophecy, to another distinguishing between spirits, to another speaking in different kinds of tongues, and to still another the interpretation of tongues. All these are the work of one and the same Spirit, and he gives them to each one, just as he determines. (1 Cor. 12:7–11)

The End. The apostle John's account of the end of time was received in the presence and power of the Holy Spirit: "On the Lord's Day I was in the Spirit" (Rev. 1:10). While in the Spirit, he encountered each person of the Trinity and came face-to-face with a vision of the last days of humanity. The Holy Spirit spoke to the church and about the eternal blessings of those who die in the Lord: "Then I heard a voice from heaven say, 'Write: Blessed are the dead who die in the Lord from now on.' 'Yes,' says the Spirit, 'they will rest from their labor, for their deeds will follow them'" (Rev. 14:13).

The great lesson for the church and for the individual Christian is the same and is best stated by Jesus himself while speaking to the apostle John: "He who has an ear, let him hear what the Spirit says to the churches" (Rev. 2:7).

The Exercise

Look at the following verses, and determine which ones speak to the Deity (D), Personhood (P), and Trinity (T) of the Holy Spirit:

- Acts 5:3–4   D   P   T
- Matthew 3:16   D   P   T
- John 16:7–8   D   P   T
- Ephesians 1:17   D   P   T
- Hebrews 10:29   D   P   T
- 1 John 3:23–24   D   P   T
- 2 Corinthians 13:14   D   P   T
- 1 Thessalonians 5:19   D   P   T
- Ephesians 4:30   D   P   T
- Jude 20–21   D   P   T
- Romans 8:26–27   D   P   T
- Acts 7:51   D   P   T
- Acts 10:19–21   D   P   T

6
The Holy Bible

God speaks to

us through his

Word, the Bible,

to tell us of him

and lead us

to him.

The Conversation

"Where did the Bible come from?"

With the newfound interest in all of the conspiracy theories about who decided which books are in the Bible and why they chose the ones they did, this question is more common than ever.

There are two kinds of conversations you will encounter on this topic. First are those who will initiate a conversation on this topic because they are looking for a way to discredit your faith. Those with such motives may have several kinds of arguments on this point. They may bring up questions about the Gnostic gospels that were written three hundred years after Jesus' death and resurrection. They may bring up questions about the political motivations to choose certain writings over others. They may dwell on conspiracy theories about the origins of the Bible. When discrediting the faith is the motive, just politely bring an end to the conversation and then discuss football or the weather. Don't argue. That will only escalate the emotion and is not at all likely to lead to any sort of breakthrough. Just move on.

But for others, the question is sincere. There is a real desire to understand the origins of a faith they have chosen to take seriously. With these intentions behind the question, this can be a great conversation. You may be thinking, "I could never memorize enough stuff to have that conversation." But you can. The truth presented in this chapter is not all about dates and names of authors. It is about the validity of the Scriptures of our faith. You can have this conversation. And your friends who are genuinely interested will be better off because you did.

Teachable Questions

Who wrote the Bible?

Who chose which books would be in the Bible?

How did they make that choice?

Where did the Old and New Testaments come from?

How are the Old and New Testaments different?

What is the extra part, the Apocrypha, that is in the Catholic Bible?

How much should I let the Bible influence me?

Is the Bible really the word of God?

Is the Bible reliable?

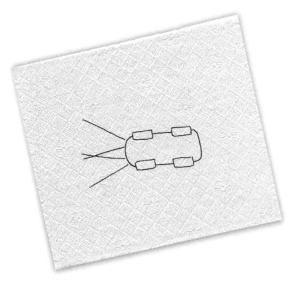

The Napkin

The Bible is God's word (truth) for all mankind. It is the light that shows us the way to God. Just like the headlights on our cars light our paths as we drive down the road at night, the Word of God, the Bible, lights our way as we walk through this world. And let's be honest: this world can be very dark and directionless.

Making decisions without God's Word is like driving at night on a curvy mountain road without headlights. It just isn't wise.

We should never make a move in life without the illuminating insight of God's Word. God gives us insight and direction through the Bible that can keep us safe and show us the right way to go. We would be wise to take advantage of it.

The Truth

> For you have been born again, not of perishable seed, but of imperishable, through the living and enduring word of God. For, "all men are like grass and their glory is like the flowers of the field; the grass withers and the flowers fall, but the word of the Lord stands forever." And this is the word that was preached to you.
> —1 Peter 1:23–25

Every religion has its own set of sacred writings. For Christianity, those writings are contained within the pages of the Holy Bible. The Bible is a collection of sixty-six writings from forty-four different authors composed over a period of fifteen hundred years. It is generally accepted that the thirty-nine books of the Old Testament were written between 1400 and 400 B.C. The twenty-seven books of the New Testament are believed to have been written between A.D. 50 and 100. The continuity and consistency of these writings with each other over such a long period of human history is one of the key arguments for the validity of the Holy Bible.

Needless to say, there are those who question this. Some question authorship and dates of composition, while others question the methods used in selecting the actual writings included. It should be noted that any document of historical origin is debated as to its meaning, interpretation, and accuracy. The Holy Bible is no exception.

The Canon of Scripture

The canon of the Bible is the list of those books which meet the standard and are worthy of inclusion in this compilation of sacred texts. Both the Old and New Testaments have been through periods of debate which have established a canon (listing) of authoritative and accepted texts.

The Old Testament Canon

The Old Testament canon was firmly established around 165 B.C. At that point, the entire collection of the Old Testament was seen as authoritative by a wide majority of the Jewish community. Prior to this, the Old Testament had been accepted in basically three different time frames: the Pentateuch, the Prophets, and the hagiographa.

The Pentateuch or the books of the Law (Genesis, Exodus, Leviticus, Numbers, and Deuteronomy) were the first to be universally accepted. The Samaritans never accepted any writings outside of the Pentateuch.

The Prophets include the historical books of Joshua, Judges, 1 and 2 Samuel, and 1 and 2 Kings, as well as the prophetic writings of Jeremiah, Ezekiel, Isaiah, Hosea, Joel, Amos, Obadiah, Jonah, Micah, Nahum, Habakkuk, Zephaniah, Haggai, Zechariah, and Malachi.

The hagiographa or sacred writings include Job, Psalms, Proverbs, Ecclesiastes, Song of Songs (or Solomon), Ruth, Lamentations, Esther, Daniel, 1 and 2 Chronicles, Ezra, and Nehemiah.

The Apocrypha or "hidden things" are writings that are included in some versions of the Bible, including Roman Catholic Bible versions. The books of the Apocrypha are not accepted by Protestants as Scripture. However, many consider them valuable for historical and other purposes. The books listed in the Catholic Apocrypha are Tobias, Judith, the Wisdom of Solomon, Baruch, and 1 and 2 Maccabees. There are other books listed in the Old Testament or Jewish Apocrypha and still more have been listed by different scholars at different times. There is no shortage of writing about the history of Israel and the life of Jesus the Christ. And while the early church leaders did not view most of these writings as rising to the level of Scripture, they did view many of them as acceptable and recommended supplemental reading.

The New Testament Canon

The New Testament canon was finalized at the Council of Carthage in A.D. 397. Although this seems a late date for a final accounting of the books of the New Testament, general agreement on much of the New Testament came much earlier. In fact, there were versions of the New Testament being translated into Latin, Syriac, and Coptic languages as early as A.D. 200.

By the late fourth century, the debate had become fairly limited, and by the time of the Council of Carthage, the discussion came down to the following two categories:

1. Universal acceptance was given to Matthew, Mark, Luke, John, Acts, Romans, 1 and 2 Corinthians, Galatians, Ephesians, Philippians, Colossians, 1 and 2 Thessalonians, 1 and 2 Timothy, Titus, Philemon, Hebrews, 1 Peter, 1 John, and Revelation.
2. Admitted by the majority but still under some debate were James, 2 Peter, 2 and 3 John, and Jude.

Therefore, of the twenty-seven writings contained in today's New Testament, only five were under further consideration at the Council of Carthage. The church was clear in its establishment of the canon of the Holy Bible.

The New Testament is divided into four major sections.

1. The Gospels—the accounts of the life of Jesus
2. The Acts of the Apostles
3. The Epistles—twenty-one letters written by apostles and "apostolic men"
4. The Revelation

Although other "gospels" and "epistles" have been brought forward over the centuries and suggested as viable scriptures, the church has remained firm in its acceptance of this sixty-six book canon of the Holy Scriptures.

The Authority of Scripture

Today we follow the authority of Scripture for decisions we make in our lives, society, and the church. The apostle Paul again captured our understanding of God and his word when he wrote to Timothy, "All Scripture is God-breathed and is useful for teaching, rebuking, correcting, and training in righteousness, so that the man of God may be thoroughly equipped for every good work" (2 Tim. 3:16–17).

The Inspiration of Scripture

> The Law of the LORD is perfect, reviving the soul. The statutes of the LORD are trustworthy, making wise the simple. The precepts of the LORD are right, giving joy to the heart. The commands of the LORD are radiant, giving light to the eyes. The fear of the LORD is pure, enduring forever. The ordinances of the LORD are sure and altogether righteous.
> —Psalm 19:7–9

The term *God-breathed* that the apostle Paul used is significant in our understanding of Scripture. The modern theologian J. I. Packer put it this way, "The thought is not of God as breathing out God, but of God as having breathed out Scripture. Paul's words mean, not that Scripture is inspiring (true though it is), but that Scripture is a divine product and must be approached and estimated as such."[1] Scripture is, in the end, the divine word of God. His *logos* or truth or knowledge is imparted to us through the Bible. But take care of a major mistake that some make: Some would say that God's Word becomes truth for me when I accept it. Not so. God's Word *is* truth and life, and it *is* inspired—even when I or anyone else refuses to accept it. The Holy Bible does not need our acceptance to become truth. The Holy Bible receives our acceptance because it *is* truth.

Inerrancy vs. Infallibility

While there are some who question the validity of Scripture at every point, most biblical scholars do not. However, even among those who hold the validity of Scripture in high regard, there is debate over the meaning of two words:

- *Inerrancy*—the belief that the original manuscripts, if found, would be without any error of any kind.
- *Infallibility*—the belief that the teaching of the Bible is entirely unfailing even though certain factual or grammatical errors may exist.

It is not my desire to spend a great deal of time here debating between inerrancy and infallibility. Both of these views take the truth of Scripture seriously and that seems to me to be the real issue. While I realize that this answer will not suffice for some, this is not the place for a larger discussion on the issue.

The Usefulness of Scripture

> For the word of God is living and active. Sharper than any double-edged sword, it penetrates even to dividing soul and spirit, joints and marrow; it judges the thoughts and attitudes of the heart.
> —Hebrews 4:12

If we truly believe that the Holy Bible is the Logos, or Word, of God, then we should take the insights and instruction found there seriously. As the apostle Paul pointed out, this "God-breathed" Word is useful for "teaching, rebuking, correcting and training in righteousness" (2 Tim. 3:16). In other words, we should allow this Scripture to determine the direction and outcome of our daily lives. We should allow it to teach us about life, God, people, and eternity. We should accept from the Holy Scriptures rebuke and correction so that things in our lives that do not match the level of righteousness presented in Scripture are cleansed and changed. We should learn from the training that is offered here and apply that training in our everyday living. In the end, the good news of God's Word should develop within us a righteousness that was not there before. The apostle goes on to say that Scripture is given "so that the man of God may be thoroughly equipped for every good work" (2 Tim. 3:17). In other words, we should become someone we were not in the beginning. The truth is that when we first found faith in Christ, we were not equipped for the life of righteousness that God intended for us. It is through the work of the Word in the life of the believer that God changes us from the lostness in which we began to the powerful life of holiness he desires for us. The power of God's Word changes our lives.

The Exercise

Consider the following verses, and write down what they say about God's Word:

- John 8:32
- 2 Peter 1:20–21
- Matthew 24:35
- 2 Timothy 3:14–15
- Revelation 22:18–19

For the wages of sin is death, but the gift of God
is eternal life in Christ Jesus our Lord.
—Romans 6:23

7
The Gospel

Jesus, on the

cross of Calvary,

paid the price

for our sinfulness

and provided

forgiveness.

The Conversation

"What does it mean when Christians say I need to be saved?" Or, "What do people mean when they say I need to be born again?"

These are great questions! Christians long to hear questions like these from their friends. When people ask, it generally means that they are ready to consider a deeper life-changing relationship with Jesus Christ.

Now, for some Christians, these questions can cause real fear. When we do not feel prepared to answer, we can fear failure and find ourselves hoping that no one will ask. But you don't have to live with that fear. The offer of salvation is not difficult to explain. The graphic on the next page gives you plenty of information to share. You can learn a simple way to lead those around you to the Savior you already know. And then when you hear one of these questions, you will feel the excitement of knowing that a life is about to change for the better!

Teachable Questions

What does it mean to be saved?

Why do I need to be saved?

What do I need to be saved from?

How can Jesus help me?

Why did Jesus have to die?

What did the cross accomplish?

Why do I feel so distant from God?

Why do I feel guilty around Christians?

How can I know God?

How can I know I am a Christian?

The Napkin

The drawing for this chapter also forms the basis for this chapter and also the next. It illustrates the theology of what Jesus accomplished on the cross.

Very little debate is needed to establish the fact that mankind is tainted by some sort of evil. Even if we accept the fact that people are generally good, we are forced to pause and admit that every human being has made wrong choices, bad decisions, and even acted in evil ways.

We are all caught in this together.

The grand questions for philosophers, theologians, and all human beings are profound: Is there a way out of this sin and evil? Who has the authority to forgive this sin and evil? Who can do anything about it?

The gospel, or good news is the announcement that Jesus can and will deal with the sin and evil within the hearts of individual human beings.

The Truth

The Gap

"God saw all that he had made, and it was very good" (Gen. 1:31).

God created mankind to have a relationship of perfect friendship with himself. Humanity was to manage and care for the garden of Eden and its inhabitants. God spent time with the man and woman, and he would come and take walks with Adam and Eve "in the cool of the day" (Gen. 3:8). But all of this beauty was interrupted by the introduction of sin into the world of humanity. When Adam and Eve decided to disobey God's direct command to stay away from the Tree of Knowledge of Good and Evil (Gen. 2:15–17; 3:1–7), the result was a separation from God that was not the original desire of the Creator. From that point on, humanity has been tainted by the existence of sin in the human race. Fortunately, God's desire for a relationship with mankind did not end after Adam's failure in the garden. Let's take a look at the events of human history from Adam's sin to Jesus' redemption.

God Is from the Beginning

"In the beginning God created the heavens and the earth. Now the earth was formless and empty, darkness was over the surface of the deep, and the Spirit of God was hovering over the waters" (Gen. 1:1–2).

God Is in Fellowship with Man

"Then God said, 'Let us make man in our image, in our likeness, and let them rule over the fish of the sea and the birds of the air, over the livestock, over all the earth, and over all the creatures that move along the ground.' So God created man in his own image, in the image of God he created him; male and female he created them" (Gen. 1:26–27).

Sin Separates Man from God

"So the LORD God banished him from the Garden of Eden to work the ground from which he had been taken. After he drove the man out, he placed on the east side of the Garden of Eden cherubim and a flaming sword flashing back and forth to guard the way to the tree of life" (Gen. 3:23–24).

Jesus Bridges the Gap between Man and God

Therefore, there is now no condemnation for those who are in Christ Jesus, because through Christ Jesus the law of the Spirit of life set me free from the law of sin and death. For what the law was powerless to do in that it was weakened by the sinful nature,

God did by sending his own Son in the likeness of sinful man to be a sin offering. And so he condemned sin in sinful man, in order that the righteous requirements of the law might be fully met in us, who do not live according to the sinful nature but according to the Spirit. (Rom. 8:1–4)

Jesus Restores Relationship with God and Man

"Now there have been many of those priests, since death prevented them from continuing in office; but because Jesus lives forever, he has a permanent priesthood. Therefore he is able to save completely those who come to God through him, because he always lives to intercede for them" (Heb. 7:23–25).

The Exercise

Read the following verses, and write down what you see in them regarding the state of man and the role of God:

- Romans 5:8
- Ephesians 2:1–10
- Galatians 4:1–7
- 1 Corinthians 6:9–11
- John 3:16–18

For it is by grace you have been saved,
through faith—and this not from yourselves,
it is the gift of God.
—Ephesians 2:8

8
Grace

God loves us so much
that he gives us his
presence and offers
his forgiveness when
we absolutely do
not deserve it!

The Conversation

"Since I know I don't deserve God's forgiveness or his help, how can I expect that he will forgive me or help me in my life?"

This is a great question. Most people realize that there is a lot of sin in the world and that something needs to be done about all of it. But most people still seem to believe that all sin is someone else's problem. We all face times when we fail to understand our own shortcomings and failures, but then there are other times when we realize who we really are and the problems we actually have. At those moments, we can find ourselves not so sure why God would ever choose to forgive us. We are not even sure we would or could forgive ourselves. And somehow we expect the God of heaven to forgive us, help us, journey with us, and ultimately change us?

But he does! And that is the good news of a thing we call grace. When people realize their need for the grace of God, they find themselves in the perfect place to experience the life-changing presence of God in their lives! And you can help them understand how much God really loves us all—so much that he would give us the forgiveness and help that we absolutely do not deserve.

Teachable Questions

How is it that people just seem to know they need God?

Why is it that almost everybody believes that there is a God?

What is it that draws me to God in the first place?

How can I ever hope to be more like God?

How can I ever believe that a holy God would choose to help me?

Does the Bible really say that God cares about helping me change?

The Napkin

The drawing for this chapter appeared first in the previous chapter. It illustrates the theology of what Jesus accomplished on the cross.

Grace is defined as unmerited favor.

In other words, grace is forgiveness or blessing that we do not deserve but that is given to us anyway. Grace is most often displayed to us by people who love us. They may choose to help us when we do not deserve their help or forgive us when we do not deserve their forgiveness. This is grace.

The good news is that God has shown just that kind of grace to us. By loving us enough to send Jesus to pay the price for our salvation, God has displayed his grace. But that grace actually began long before we were ready to hear about it. God's grace has been extended to us our entire lives.

The Truth

The Grace to Seek God

> No one can come to me unless the
> Father who sent me draws him.
> —John 6:44

Sin has left mankind so hopelessly lost that there is no possible way that any of us would even think to come to God on our own. For that reason, God has allowed grace to preside over all of mankind so that we can sense and respond to his leading us toward himself. This grace is called prevenient grace, or a grace that comes before salvation. Without this prevenient grace, we would never have any hope of coming to the Lord for the forgiveness of our sins and the correction of our lost state.

The Grace to Find God

> But I, when I am lifted up from the earth,
> will draw all men to myself.
> —John 12:32

The prevenient grace of God allows us to sense his presence, hear his call, and respond to his love for us. But in the end, the final choice is ours. As the Holy Spirit draws us to the cross of Christ for our forgiveness, we must decide if we are going to accept his love for us and find forgiveness, or reject his love and continue on in our lost state of sin. The truth is that some choose to remain in sin even when the free gift of eternal life and salvation is offered. The actual act of receiving God's grace for our lives is not difficult.

The Grace to Receive God

I suggest the following four-step prayer to receive God's salvation in your life:

Confess. Admit that you have sinned. "For all have sinned and fall short of the glory of God" (Rom. 3:23).

Believe. Jesus can and will forgive your sins. "For the wages of sin is death but the gift of God is eternal life through Jesus Christ our Lord" (Rom. 6:23).

Repent. Change your ways to his ways. "Repent, then, and turn to God, so that your sins may be wiped out, that times of refreshing may come from the Lord" (Acts 3:19).

Receive. Accept his love for you. "If you confess with your mouth, 'Jesus is Lord,' and believe in your heart that God raised him from the dead, you will be saved" (Rom. 10:9).

> For it is by grace you have been saved, through faith—and this not from yourselves, it is the gift of God—not by works, so that no one can boast.
> —Ephesians 2:8–9

The Grace to Pursue God

> So I find this law at work: When I want to do good, evil is right there with me. For in my inner being I delight in God's law; but I see another law at work in the members of my body, waging war against the law of my mind and making me a prisoner of the law of sin at work within my members. What a wretched man I am! Who will rescue me from this body of death? Thanks be to God—through Jesus Christ our Lord!
> —Romans 7:21–25

The next step in our experience of God's grace is to grow in that grace to begin becoming more like him. It is again only the power of grace that allows growth to take place in our lives. Without God's grace, we would have no hope of ever doing anything of worth. However, in the grace of God, we can find the ability to live differently and better. We can find the ability to choose more wisely—the righteous things in life over the sinful things that have controlled us for so long. Often this battle within us can seem overwhelming and hopeless. While we work and strive to do the good things that God has called us to, it seems that our sinful hearts just continually run back into the sin and trouble that God delivered us from. But there is good news even in that struggle. Grace brings change. And ultimately grace brings heart change that will lead to a change in choices and actions.

The Grace to Desire God

> I know that nothing good lives in me, that is, in my sinful nature. For I have the desire to do what is good, but I cannot carry it out.
> —Romans 7:18

> You were taught, with regard to your former way of life, to put off your old self, which is being corrupted by its deceitful desires; to be made new in the attitude of your minds; and to put on the new self, created to be like God in true righteousness and holiness.
> —Ephesians 4:22–24

What we want in our Christian life is not that God would just force us to change our actions. Ultimately we want God to change our desires. We need the Holy

Spirit to take over our lives to the point that what God wants for us is what we want to do. We call this process sanctification, or being set apart for holy purposes. Every Christian should be growing toward a deeper experience of sanctification. There must come a time in Christian life that every part of us is surrendered to the control and direction of the Holy Spirit. Until we reach that place of total surrender, we are living in less than God's best for us. Let's be clear: We are saved by faith alone. But that faith will come with a life that is changed inside and out. To accomplish this state of holy living, we need God to change our desires from those that are natural to us to those that are natural to him.

No one who is born of God will continue to sin, because God's seed remains in him; he cannot go on sinning, because he has been born of God. This is how we know who the children of God are and who the children of the devil are: Anyone who does not do what is right is not a child of God; nor is anyone who does not love his brother.
—1 John 3:9–10

The Exercise

Consider the following verses, and write down how the grace of God should make our lives different.

- James 2:8
- Ephesians 2:10
- John 15:5–8
- Philippians 2:1–4
- Matthew 5:16
- 1 Peter 1:13–16
- James 2:18

Jesus replied, "Blessed are you, Simon son of Jonah, for this was not revealed to you by man, but by my Father in heaven. And I tell you that you are Peter, and on this rock I will build my church, and the gates of Hades will not overcome it."
—Matthew 16:17–18

9
The Church

The church is the body of Christ here on earth. That body is made up of a collection of redeemed believers who gather to worship, learn from, experience, and serve Christ together.

The Conversation

"Since I am a Christian, do I have to go to church every week?"

I have been asked this question in different forms many times over the years. But the answer is always the same: Yes! A Christian asking if he must go to church is like a football fan asking if he must go to the game. True fans never ask that question. If they can get to the game and watch their team play, they go.

As I have pointed out in other chapters, some who ask this question are not doing so out of an honest search for truth. Some people ask the question and then start debating with you, not because they want to reach understanding, but because they don't want to go to church. And these people are just working to start an argument. If you get frustrated with the argument, say some things you wish you hadn't said, and huff out in anger, they will probably say, "If that is the way church people act, I don't need to go there." And so, as I have said before, if you find yourself in this type of conversation, politely end it and start talking about something else.

But for those looking for understanding, the church does have purpose and meaning. You can be the one God uses to help someone understand what that purpose and meaning is.

Teachable Questions

Do Christians have to go to church?

What is the purpose of the church?

Where did the idea of church come from?

What should we be doing at church?

Does the church really make a difference in society?

Does the Bible really tell us to go to church?

Is the church an important part of society in general?

What does the church provide to the culture around us?

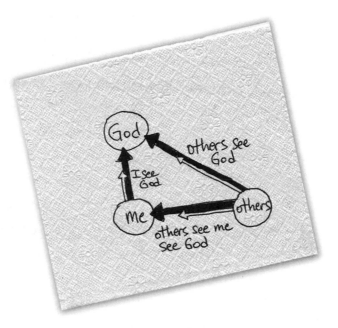

The Napkin

The work of the church is fairly simple to explain.
We see God. Others see us seeing God. Others see God.
The world around us should see our worship, service,
and devotion to God and ultimately see him through us.
That is the work of the body of Christ here on earth.

If they see us seeing God, they will wonder.

If they see us seeing God, they will search.

If they see us seeing God, they can see him.

If they see us seeing God, they can receive him.

The History of the Assembly of God's People

Throughout the history of mankind, God's people have gathered to worship him. Some today have argued that the church has no real significance in modern life. Some are arguing for the end of what they would call organized religion, saying that there is no scriptural mandate for such a gathering of the believers.

Let me be clear—they are wrong.

The church, defined as either all those individuals who are followers of Christ or defined as those followers of Christ who gather corporately for the worship of God, is ordained, established, and commanded by Scripture. This is a matter of dogma.

The first time we see large numbers of God's people able to gather for corporate worship is in the book of Exodus. As Moses led the children of Israel, then becoming the nation of Israel, out of captivity in Egypt and toward freedom and the Promised Land, God commanded the building of a structure that would serve as the central gathering point for the people of God to gather for the worship of God. "Then have them make a sanctuary for me, and I will dwell among them" (Ex. 25:8). God then established this gathering place as his tool for leading his people. "In all the travels of the Israelites, whenever the cloud lifted from above the tabernacle, they would set out; but if the cloud did not lift, they did not set out—until the day it lifted. So the cloud of the Lord was over the tabernacle by day, and fire was in the cloud by night, in the sight of all the house of Israel during all their travels" (Ex. 40:36–38).

> Then the king called together all the elders of Judah and Jerusalem. He went up to the temple of the Lord with the men of Judah, the people of Jerusalem, the priests and the prophets—all the people from the least to the greatest. He read in their hearing all the words of the Book of the Covenant, which had been found in the temple of the Lord.
> —2 Kings 23:1–2

Once the nation of Israel was firmly established in the land that God had promised them, God directed King Solomon to carry out the wishes of his father, King David, and build a permanent place of worship, the temple. After its completion, God blessed this new gathering place with his presence. "When the priests withdrew from the Holy Place, the cloud filled the temple of the Lord. And the priests could not perform their service because of the cloud, for the glory of the Lord filled his temple" (1 Kings 8:10–11).

From this time on, whenever God's people needed to hear his voice, they would gather together at the temple (God's house) to worship and cry out to him. From the temple, kings, priests, and prophets would declare the word of the Lord and the people of God would worship him and offer sacrifices to him. The temple was the centerpiece of, not only Jewish religious life, but Jewish cultural life as well.

> They went to Capernaum, and when the
> Sabbath came, Jesus went into the
> synagogue and began to teach.
> —Mark 1:21

The time came when the temple was destroyed, but the gathering of God's people did not end with the destruction of the temple. A new gathering place emerged called the synagogue. Here the Israelites gathered to worship God and hear the Scriptures read and explained. Again, the gathering place for the worship of God became the centerpiece of Jewish life. And when Jesus, and later the apostles, began to teach about new life through a risen Messiah, it was in the synagogue that this gospel of redemption was first preached.

> Every day they continued to meet together in
> the temple courts. They broke bread in their
> homes and ate together with glad and sincere
> hearts, praising God and enjoying the favor of
> all the people. And the Lord added to their
> number daily those who were being saved.
> —Acts 2:46–47

From the very beginning of Christianity, the church would gather together for worship and Scripture reading and training. There was no question among the early Christians as to whether or not they should meet in corporate worship; they just knew they should. There was no concern for the size of the group; they met in both large and small groups. The issue was that the people of God gather for the worship of God and for the teaching of his word. It has been so at least since the days of Moses. Those who would decide today, some four thousand years later, that it is not really necessary, fall into nothing less than heresy.

The Purpose of the Assembly of God's People

> Let us hold unswervingly to the hope we profess, for he who promised is faithful. And let us consider how we may spur one another on toward love and good deeds. Let us not give up meeting together, as some are in the habit of doing, but let us encourage one another—and all the more as you see the Day approaching.
> —Hebrews 10:23–25

The Church Establishes Hope. God has always used his people to bring hope to a hurting world. The church today is no different. It is the call of today's church to declare the Word of God to people who would otherwise not hear his truth, preach the good news of salvation through Christ Jesus, and demonstrate the power of the

Holy Spirit to the world around us. It may be true that some churches and Christians are not effectively accomplishing this task and are actually showing the world a skewed and even wrong view of God, the Scriptures, and Christianity. Nevertheless, the truth is the truth. God has always ordained his church to declare his truth to the world. In doing so, we make the hope of eternal salvation available to the world around us.

> They devoted themselves to the apostles' teaching and to the fellowship, to the breaking of bread and to prayer. Everyone was filled with awe, and many wonders and miraculous signs were done by the apostles.
> —Acts 2:42–43

The Church Establishes Truth. Today, as never before in human history, the church must speak loudly the voice of truth. In today's world, truth is not considered a reality. Truth is seen as either nonexistent or inaccessible. And yet, God has clearly established his truth in the Scriptures and has clearly called the church, as a corporate body of believers, to declare that truth. God has, in fact, empowered the church through the Holy Spirit to declare his truth in miraculous ways. The strength of the church is not found in the simple gathering of people. The strength is found in that those people who gather devote themselves to his truth together. Too many believers and churches have given up on the truth of

Scripture while trying to maintain the gathering of the saints. Without Scripture, there are no saints. Without truth, there is no Holy Spirit power. Without Holy Spirit power, there is no church.

> Consequently, you are no longer foreigners and aliens, but fellow citizens with God's people and members of God's household, built on the foundation of the apostles and prophets, with Christ Jesus himself as the chief cornerstone. In him the whole building is joined together and rises to become a holy temple in the Lord. And in him you too are being built together to become a dwelling in which God lives by his Spirit.
> —Ephesians 2:19–22

The Church Establishes Community. Community is rapidly disappearing in modern culture. We have become a society of isolated individuals with no real connection to the world around us. We find our social outlets in all the wrong places. People go to bars, the Internet, or out-of-control parties to find some sense of community. Until recent generations, the church has often been the center of community life. And while it seems that this is not true today, the church still plays a vital role in every community. That role may not be taken seriously by some in our society, and may even be taken for granted by some in the church, but its importance cannot be denied. If we are honest with ourselves and our understanding of Western civilization, it is not

Western civilization that formed Christianity or the church. It is Christianity and the church that has formed Western civilization. Before the church and before the gospel of Christ, societies that exist in freedom and democracy like we know now could not have been imagined. Even today, societies that lack the underpinnings of Christianity find freedom and democracy difficult concepts. Christ and his church have established a society of community that is capable of becoming a community of peace.

The Exercise

Look at the following verses, and write down the work of the church you find there:

- Acts 2:42–47
- Matthew 18:15–17
- Acts 12:5
- 1 Corinthians 12:12–31
- 1 Corinthians 16:1–2
- James 5:13–16
- Acts 14:21–23
- Matthew 28:18–20

But just as he who called you is holy, so be holy in all you do; for it is written: "Be holy, because I am holy."

—1 Peter 1:15–16

10

Sanctification

God not only
chooses to save
us, but he
also chooses to
change us!

The Conversation

"OK, I asked Jesus to forgive me; now when will I actually change?"

That is a great question! There is often a frustration among newer Christians when it comes to the issue of being changed. While we realize that we are forgiven, we also realize that we have not completely changed.

We still struggle and fail in our attempts to follow Jesus. So the question is a good one. When do we actually change?

Further, *how* do we actually change? The answer is found in the word *sanctification*. While I will explain in more detail later, sanctification is surrender. We are not looking for victory over sin nearly as much as we are looking for surrender to the Holy Spirit. When we are surrendered, we change. And change is what we are after.

God says that through the Holy Spirit change is possible. If someone asks you how they are supposed to find it, don't be intimidated. You can do this. The person's life—and yours—will be better because you can.

Teachable Questions

When will my life actually be changed?

What kind of process is involved in becoming more like Jesus?

How do I get closer to God?

How does my life get cleaned up after I am saved?

What is God going to do in my life now that I know him?

Can I actually be more like Jesus?

Does God just forgive my sin, or will he also free me from sin?

I know God can forgive me, but can he change me?

I know I am a new person in grace, but can I be a new person in practice?

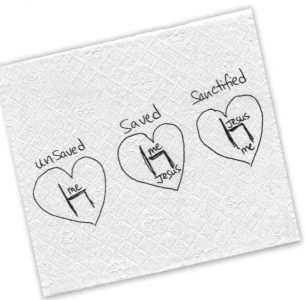

The Napkin

sanc·ti·fy: [sangk-tuh-fahy] –verb (used with object), -fied, -fy·ing.

1. to make holy; set apart as sacred; consecrate.
2. to purify or free from sin: *Sanctify your hearts.*
3. to impart religious sanction to; to render legitimate or binding: *to sanctify a vow.*
4. to entitle to reverence or respect.
5. to make productive of or conducive to spiritual blessing.[1]

Before we know God, we are firmly seated on the throne of our lives as the kings of all we do and say. We are in charge of our lives, decisions, and actions. No one else is given permission to direct or control us.

Life is controlled by me. Life is all about me.

When we receive Christ as our Savior, we allow the Holy Spirit into hearts. We surrender some of the space in our hearts to him in return for his forgiveness and grace.

While we are forgiven, we are still very much in charge.

This is a very awkward place in our Christian walk. The very Creator of the universe is living in our hearts, yet we are not allowing him to sit on the throne of our hearts. The One who occupies the throne of heaven is barred from the throne of our hearts.

This must change. While we have surrendered a little, we must give more.

When we fully surrender to the presence of the Holy Spirit in our lives, we choose to place him on the throne of our lives. This means we are fully surrendered.

He is in charge. His laws rule. His will takes over. His direction decides.

This decision to surrender is a decision to become entirely sanctified or entirely set apart for holy or sacred use. As a result, our relationship to God feels natural.

The One who sits on the throne of heaven now also sits on the throne of our lives.

We are surrendered. We are sanctified.

The Truth

Initial Sanctification (Salvation)

> Therefore, if anyone is in Christ, he is a new
> creation; the old has gone, the new has come!
> —2 Corinthians 5:17

Salvation is the initial step in sanctification.

On the day that a follower of Jesus Christ admits the need for forgiveness and surrenders to the grace and mercy of God through Jesus Christ, that believer is immediately set apart for the sacred purposes of God. That setting apart is the beginning of the work of sanctification in the life of the believer.

The apostle Paul said, "What shall we say, then? Shall we go on sinning so that grace may increase? By no means! We died to sin; how can we live in it any longer? Or don't you know that all of us who were baptized into Christ Jesus were baptized into his death? We were therefore buried with him through baptism into death in order that, just as Christ was raised from the dead through the glory of the Father, we too may live a new life" (Rom. 6:1–4).

The point here is quite clear: When we receive Jesus as our Savior, we die to our old ways of sin.

We *die* to them. Just like Jesus died on the cross for us.

And then we are raised again with him so that we can live free from all that sin for which God already forgave us. Salvation is more than just forgiveness. Salvation is freedom from sin. The same blood that washed us clean from our sin and bridged the gap of sinfulness so that we can have a restored relationship with God can empower us to live a life that is new, clean, and capable of over-coming sin.

Salvation is just the first step in that process.

Progressive Sanctification (Growing in Grace)

Again in Romans, the apostle Paul spoke to the issue of progressive sanctification.

"In the same way, count yourselves dead to sin but alive to God in Christ Jesus. Therefore do not let sin reign in your mortal body so that you obey its evil desires. Do not offer the parts of your body to sin, as instruments of wickedness, but rather offer yourselves to God, as those who have been brought from death to life; and offer the parts of your body to him as instruments of righteous-ness. For sin shall not be your master, because you are not under law, but under grace" (Rom. 6:11–14).

> Since we have these promises, dear friends, let us purify ourselves from everything that contaminates body and spirit, perfecting holiness out of reverence for God.
> —2 Corinthians 7:1

Once we have surrendered our sin in order to receive the forgiveness of God through Christ, we must surrender our actions so that we can glorify him through our lives. Before we were forgiven by Jesus, we were captives to the sin that we had struggled with all our lives. We were caught in the vicious cycle of falling down and then getting back up. Try and fail. Fail and try. And then came Jesus.

Freedom arrived, and God placed the Holy Spirit into our hearts since we had surrendered to the grace of Christ. Once the Holy Spirit entered our lives, it was his work to set us free. While Jesus set us free from the penalty of sin, it is the Holy Spirit that sets us free from the habit of sin. With the Holy Spirit in control, we now have the capacity to live differently. We have the ability to say no to the sin that once entangled us so easily. The Holy Spirit works in our lives to set us free.

As we surrender more to his leadings, we fall less into the trap of sin, and our lives therefore look more like the Christ we serve.

We are progressing toward the sanctification that God had planned for us all along.

Entire Sanctification (Complete Surrender)

May God himself, the God of peace, sanctify you through and through. May your whole spirit, soul and body be kept blameless at the coming of our Lord Jesus Christ. The one who calls you is faithful and he will do it.
—1 Thessalonians 5:23–24

There comes a point where we are faced with the choice of finally surrendering all that we are to the control and power of the Holy Spirit. At this point, we must make a choice. Who is going to finally sit on the throne of our heart?

Entire sanctification is allowing the Holy Spirit to have that place of honor and control in our life.

Paul said, "When you were slaves to sin, you were free from the control of righteousness. What benefit did you reap at that time from the things you are now ashamed of? Those things result in death! But now that you have been set free from sin and have become slaves to God, the benefit you reap leads to holiness, and the result is eternal life. For the wages of sin is death, but the gift of God is eternal life in Christ Jesus our Lord" (Rom. 6:20–23).

Paul argued that we all live as slaves to something. Some choose to live out their lives as slaves to sin that will destroy them. And we have all seen tragic examples of this kind of slavery. But God calls us to a different life. God calls us to a life lived out as slaves to the Holy Spirit.

As slaves to righteousness, we find forgiveness and deliverance. We find peace and joy. We find hope and a future.

God has called us to be fully and completely surrendered to his forgiveness and leading. In this way, we can choose to be completely set apart for sacred purposes.

Initial sanctification, or salvation, is surrender of our sin to the saving power of God's grace. Progressive sanctification is surrender of our habits to the overcoming power of the Holy Spirit. Entire sanctification is the complete surrender of ourselves to the purpose and will of God.

Sanctification is surrender.

The Exercise

Look up the following verses, and write down what they have to say about living a sanctified life:

- Romans 8:3–4
- 1 Corinthians 6:9–11
- Ephesians 4:20–24
- Colossians 3:5–11
- 1 Thessalonians 5:23–24
- 1 John 1:5–10
- Jude 24

> Brothers, we do not want you to be ignorant about those who fall asleep, or to grieve like the rest of men, who have no hope.
> —1 Thessalonians 4:13–14

11 Eternity

There is more

to this life

than this life.

The Conversation

"So, what happens when we die?"

That question can strike fear into our hearts. The truth is that most people fear death. Often when I hear a question about the afterlife, it is being asked by someone who is trying to come to grips with the fear they are feeling at the very thought of death. And they want to know if this Christianity they have chosen to accept has anything to say about this death that they fear so much.

One of the great temptations and mistakes that many people make here is to immediately start talking about end of the world prophecies. That is not what people really want to know. Many Christians do this, though, because they think that believing in a rapture means that we might not have to experience death, just a rapturous flight into heaven after the sound of a heavenly trumpet. While that is a wonderful thought, let's be honest: Most people will not get to heaven that way. The reality is that people die, and they fear that reality. So let's not disrespect that fear by suggesting they place their hope in winning some "lottery ticket" of experiencing rapture before death.

Instead, let's stick with what Scripture has to say about death. There is more than enough hope there to help soothe our fears. God knows we fear death. And so, in his Word, the Bible, he has given us just enough to reassure us that he has it all under control and we will be alright. That is what we should talk about. That is what can bring peace. We must avoid our shaky theories about a time that has not yet happened and instead, talk about his calming promises about what he has designed and already seen.

Teachable Questions

What happens when we die?

When we die, do we go straight to heaven or somewhere else?

Is God there when I die?

What will heaven be like?

What does the Bible really say about death and eternity?

Is God really going to judge everyone?

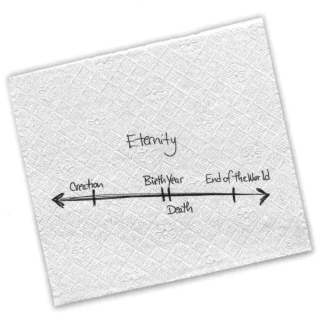

The Napkin

Eternity is literally forever.

Time is the measure we use to judge the length of our lives and our history as human beings. Time, as we know it, is like a line with two ends. The ends of this line are moving away from each other, one toward history and the other toward future.

The history end of the line continues back further than we can see or know and certainly further than we can understand or measure.

The future end of the line continues as well, moving forward further than we could even begin to imagine. It moves far beyond what we can see and is immeasurable.

If we drew a line on our napkin with arrows at each end to indicate the forever of both history and future, we could place points on it for events that we know must have occurred or must someday occur, such as creation and the end of the world as we know it.

Where would we place our birth on that line? Where would we place our death? How much of the line of eternity will our life actually cover?

And yet the Bible clearly states that we will live forever somewhere. A bit sobering isn't it?

The vast majority of our existence is in front of us, hiding in the future of eternity.

So, the most important question before us is: Where will we spend the eternity that is in front of us?

The Truth

For to me, to live is Christ and to die is gain.
If I am to go on living in the body, this will mean
fruitful labor for me. Yet what shall I choose?
I do not know! I am torn between the two:
I desire to depart and be with Christ, which
is better by far; but it is more necessary for
you that I remain in the body.
—Philippians 1:21–24

Death will overtake each of us in time. I have often stood behind a casket and gently warned families and friends that death is a reality for all human beings. In fact, although death seems to us an abnormality, it is really just the opposite. Death is normal for humans. God warned Adam and Eve in the garden that if they ate of the Tree of Knowledge of Good and Evil, they would surely die. And since that time, death has been the normal end of mankind here on earth. The good news of the gospel is that death has been defeated by Jesus on the cross. For the child of God, death is not an ending; it is a new beginning. When God allows us to slip from this earthly existence, he ushers us into our eternal heavenly existence. While death will never, and should never, be celebrated, it does not need to be feared. The ultimate end of the child of God is not a grave; it is an eternity with Jesus our Savior!

Three Views of Where We Go after Death

> Listen, I tell you a mystery: We will not all sleep,
> but we will all be changed.
> —1 Corinthians 15:51

With the Saints—Sleeping. Some have read Scripture and believe that upon our deaths we will fall into what is commonly called soul sleep. This is a state of holding that would take place between the time we die an earthly death and the time God brings us to heaven to begin our eternal life.

> The time came when the beggar died and the
> angels carried him to Abraham's side.
> —Luke 16:22

With the Saints—Waiting. Another view is that there is a holding place between earth and heaven. Some would use the word *paradise* to describe this place, and others would use the word *purgatory*. Either way what is being described is a place where the souls of those who have died before us are gathered and wait for the final judgment of God. After this judgment, those who died in Christ would enter their eternal reward.

> Jesus answered him, "I tell you the truth, today you will be with me in paradise."
> —Luke 23:43

> Therefore we are always confident and know that as long as we are at home in the body we are away from the Lord. We live by faith, not by sight. We are confident, I say, and would prefer to be away from the body and at home with the Lord.
> —2 Corinthians 5:6–8

> Do not let your hearts be troubled. Trust in God; trust also in me. In my Father's house are many rooms; if it were not so, I would have told you. I am going there to prepare a place for you. And if I go and prepare a place for you, I will come back and take you to be with me that you also may be where I am. You know the way to the place where I am going.
> —John 14:1–4

With the Savior. Still others believe that we will be immediately ushered into the presence of God upon our death. There is no holding place. There is no soul sleep. There is life on earth in the presence and power of the Holy Spirit, and then there is life in heaven in the presence and power of God the Father our Creator, Jesus our Savior, and the Holy Spirit our Sustainer.

The real issue here is that we are working to describe and understand an event that none of us has experienced. While Scripture does teach on this issue, as you have seen above, Scripture was written by Holy Spirit-inspired humans who were striving to describe the indescribable. As the apostles worked to explain the incomprehensible wonder of God's eternal love and home for us, they struggled with words that were inadequate. Therefore, we are left, to some extent, wondering. While I cannot tell you exactly what the experience will be like when we take that journey from this life to the next, I can assure you that it will be a journey filled not with fear, but with joy. In some way, God will usher us through that moment just as he has ushered us through every other in our lives. The truth is, if we know Jesus as our Savior, we are bound for heaven. Find hope in that even when you can't fully explain every detail of the journey.

Judgment

> So we make it our goal to please him, whether we are at home in the body or away from it. For we must all appear before the judgment seat of Christ, that each one may receive what is due him for the things done while in the body, whether good or bad.
> —2 Corinthians 5:9–10

> Then I saw a great white throne and him who was seated on it. Earth and sky fled from his presence, and there was no place for them. And I saw the dead, great and small, standing before the throne, and books were opened. Another book was opened, which is the book of life. The dead were judged according to what they had done as recorded in the books.
> —Revelation 20:11–12

> Then I saw a new heaven and a new earth, for the first heaven and the first earth had passed away, and there was no longer any sea. I saw the Holy City, the new Jerusalem, coming down out of heaven from God, prepared as a bride beautifully dressed for her husband. And I heard a loud voice from the throne saying, "Now the dwelling of God is with men, and he will live with them. They will be his people, and God himself will be with them and be their God. He will wipe every tear from their eyes. There will be no more death or mourning or crying or pain, for the old order of things has passed away."
> —Revelation 21:1–4

One thing we can be sure of is that God will judge each person on how his or her life was lived. While salvation is by grace alone, we will still somehow be held responsible in the next life for our actions in this life. This truth should not strike fear into the heart of a believer. It should, instead, bring a sense of thankfulness for the grace that we will be able stand in on that day. It should also bring a determination to present as godly a life for our Lord as possible. If all will be revealed and reviewed, we should be working to prepare the best review possible.

Eternal Reward

When time is done for the Christian and judgment has taken place, eternity—heavenly eternity—will begin. What eternity will be like is tough to imagine. But one thing is certain: It will be wonderful. There will be productive work to do as we rule and reign with God. There will be incredible worship in the presence of the God of the universe. It will all be different and new. But we can have confidence that it will all be better, so much better, than anything we have ever imagined.

The Exercise

List some of the descriptions of heaven that you find in Revelation 21:1—22:5.

*

*

*

•

•

•

"The angel said to me, 'These words are trustworthy and true. The Lord, the God of the spirits of the prophets, sent his angel to show his servants the things that must soon take place.' 'Behold, I am coming soon! Blessed is he who keeps the words of the prophecy in this book'" (Rev. 22:6–7).

Notes

Chapter 1
1. C. S. Lewis, *Mere Christianity* (New York: HarperCollins, 1952), 3–32.

Chapter 2
1. "Creeds and Authorized Affirmations of Faith," The Church of England, accessed May 26, 2011, http://www.churchof england.org/prayer-worship/worship/texts/newpatterns/contents/ sectione.aspx.

2. Ibid.

Chapter 4
1. "The Nicene and Constantinople Creed," Christian Classics Ethereal Library, accessed May 26, 2011, http://www.ccel.org/ ccel/schaff/hcc3.iii.xii.xiii.html.

Chapter 6
1. J. I. Packer, *"Fundamentalism" and the Word of God: Some Evangelical Principles* (Grand Rapids, Mich.: Eerdmans, 1988), 94.

Chapter 10
1. "Sanctify," Dictionary.com, accesssed November 29, 2010, http://dictionary.reference.com/browse/sanctify.

Additional Discipleship Resources

The following books are recommended resources to share with people who want to grow in their faith:

DeNeff, Steve and David Drury. *SoulShift: The Measure of a Life Transformed*. Indianapolis, Ind.: Wesleyan Publishing House, 2011.

Heer, Ken. *A Good Start: First Steps for Growing in Your New Life in Christ*. Indianapolis, Ind.: Wesleyan Publishing House, 2002.

Heer, Ken. *Your Next Step: Becoming the Person God Meant You to Be*. Indianapolis, Ind.: Wesleyan Publishing House, 2003.

Little, Paul E. *Know What You Believe*. Downers Grove, Ill.: InterVarsity Press, 2008.

McDowell, Josh. *More Than a Carpenter*. Carol Stream, Ill.: Tyndale, 2004.

Strobel, Lee. *The Case for Faith: A Journalist Investigates the Toughest Objections to Christianity*. Grand Rapids, Mich.: Zondervan, 1998.

These resources are available at www.wphonline.com.